BUILDING A LEGACY OF GENEROSITY

Transforming Your Business with Stewardship Practices

ART ZYLSTRA

Founder CFO Business Partner

BUILDING A LEGACY OF GENEROSITY
Transforming Your Business with Stewardship Practices

Printed in the United States of America

eBook ISBN: 978-1-947276-60-4
Paperback ISBN: 978-1-947276-61-1

Cover design by Laura McIntyre

Published by:
Epic Author Publishing
561-601-9871 | info@epicauthor.com https://www.EpicAuthor.com

For information contact:
Art Zylstra, 425-931-3430 artz@cfobusinesspartner.com
http://stewardingyourbusiness.com

Dedication

Many people have influenced and impacted my life in various ways. Each of these people have played a part in shaping and molding me to be the person I am today. There is not room on this page to acknowledge them all.

To my parents, Clarence and Theresa Zylstra, for instilling in me a work ethic and a desire to volunteer in the community.

To my wife, Ronda Zylstra, for her patience with me as I travelled, got my degrees, volunteered, all while we raised three children.

To my children, Clayton, Kari, and Laura for helping me to be a better parent.

Thank you to my daughter, Laura McIntyre, for coming alongside me as a marketing and technology guru to free up my time to write this book.

To Bakke Graduate University for giving me the words and inspiration to build on my stewardship theme.

Contents

Chapter 1 – Achieving Sustainable Generosity

> *"Gentleness, self-sacrifice and generosity are the exclusive possession of no one race or religion".*
> *Mahatma Gandhi*

Generosity, Stewardship, and Sustainability

What makes a business successful? Most business owners define success as being profitable. They would likely add additional goals and dreams for their business to better define success for them.

Success could mean reaching a certain dollar level of sales, a certain number of customers, or entering national or international markets. Drilling down even further, they may add paying employees above market rate or have a net profit dollar amount or percentage of sales as a target of success. Some business owners may consider a zero-carbon emission as a mark of success. Indeed, carrying out the organization's mission by solving a problem or pain in the marketplace would be a success. My role as a CFO is to help measure and report the level of success that each company is looking to achieve.

As I consider success, infusing humanity and generosity into any relationship you build, personal or professional, represents success. This simple principle seldom crosses the mind of owners as a measurement of success. Consider that this golden rule of business has proven itself repeatedly. Companies worth millions have emerged due to the generosity of individuals who facilitated critical introductions between essential partners and investors. Small start-ups grow into multi-billion-dollar businesses because employees generously care about customers and even go the extra mile for them, and, by doing so, build long-lasting advocacy for the brand. Many small businesses create sustainability and success in their communities by being generous and treating others with respect. This not only leads to business success but also personal growth and fulfillment, as you see the positive impact you can make in the world through your business.

Emily Johnson is the CEO of Johnson LLC, a small family-owned manufacturing company led by a second-generation family member. Over the years, the company has built a reputation for its quality products and commitment to the community.

Like many businesses, Johnson LLC has faced an ever-changing market landscape. More recently, global competition has become a challenge and threatens its financial sustainability. Emily knew that changes needed to be made to remain profitable.

Innovation and adapting to evolving market demands would become transformative journeys. Emily understood that to remain competitive, the company would need to embrace technology and automation. Balancing the need to reduce costs and maintain quality was achieved!

The company's next step was to study the market and identify what the consumer sought. Environmentally friendly products and customizable options were becoming market drivers. E-commerce drove sales of many small businesses, and Emily decided to take the plunge. Customers, both near and far, could now purchase their products.

Johnson LLC has always been involved in the local community, and Emily did not want to lose its support because of all the changes. She helped start a campaign called "Buy Local, Support Local." The initiative encouraged the community to purchase locally made products and services. Local businesses, in turn, pledged to source materials from local businesses as well.

Emily's next step was to implement a new financial management system. She knew how important it is to track sales, costs, and expenses in real-time. A system that allowed better, more informed decisions was crucial for monitoring the company's financial health. Having experienced the ups and downs of the economy, Emily also created a contingency fund to safeguard against unexpected expenses, emergencies, and economic downturns.

Innovation and automation were instrumental in Johnson LLC's growth, but it was Emily's commitment to generosity and sustainability that truly set the company apart. She prioritized the company's reputation in the community, operating with integrity and fairness. Emily provided fair wages and invested in employee development and training. She engaged in community initiatives and activities and encouraged employees to do the same. These actions, rooted in the principles of generosity and sustainability, not only helped the company thrive but also fostered a positive work culture and community relationships.

While the above story is fictional, it represents the desire and vision of many small businesses throughout the United States. Within the contemporary business landscape, the principles of building a profitable business through fairness and generosity are being increasingly accepted and acknowledged for their importance in crafting a vibrant and flourishing business. Integrating these principles into everyday practices can stimulate a more enriching work culture while triggering significant benefits for businesses.

Stewarding Profits, People, Partners and Places

Many of us know the phrase 'the triple bottom line.' This phrase was first coined in 1994 by John Elkington, the founder of a British consultancy called SustainAbility. He argued that companies should prepare three different (entirely separate) bottom lines. The triple bottom line (TBL) consists of three Ps: profit, people, and planet. This triple bottom line concept is the basis of the four principles of stewardship I have developed and advocated for stewardship of profits, people, partners, and places. When a business focuses on these four stewardship principles, generosity and sustainability will be the outcome. This book will dive deep into each of these stewardship principles, providing you with the knowledge and insights to build a culture of stewardship in your business environment.

Business schools often prioritize training on achieving profits, but what is often overlooked is the question of how much profit is enough. Stewarding profits is not about constantly seeking ways to increase profit margins. For true sustainability, a business must be profitable, but it's important to remember that today's business environment suggests that the more profitable a company is, the more successful it is. This success, however, is not just about financial gains. It's about the impact a business has on its people and the planet. In other words, success is a factor of both sustainability and generosity, and businesses that embrace these principles are more likely to thrive in the long run.

A successful business generates enough profits to pay the owner/shareholder a fair return on their investment. For sustainability, a company must maintain sufficient working capital to cover payroll, extend customer credit, and stock up on necessary inventory. Funds are also allocated for reinvestment in the business, allowing for the acquisition of tangible assets, technological upgrades, and the provision for unexpected contingencies. These actions should have clear goals and metrics set up to track the success of attaining these goals. By following these practices, a business is engaging in stewardship of profits.

Business stewardship goes beyond making sure there are adequate funds for sustainability. As a business owner, you have the power to shape the culture of your company. Within the profitability structure, you should think about what the stewardship of the people working for the company looks like. Unless you are a solopreneur, most businesses have employees who either help the company carry out its mission or detract from that mission. You, as the owner, must recognize employees as key stakeholders within the industry, a point that cannot be emphasized enough. Think about your interaction with peers in your circle of influence. How do you want to be treated? Are you more likely to reach out to and be friends with people who treat you with respect? That acknowledges you for the intrinsic value of who you are. By fostering a culture of stewardship, you empower your employees and yourself to contribute to the success and sustainability of your business.

Stewardship of your employees follows the same fundamental concept. Respect for each person is critical for a company to flourish.

Acknowledged as valuable, no matter what function they perform within the company. Investment in their growth as employees and people will provide multiple returns. Giving them opportunities to make important decisions about the area of work they are most involved in will generate goodwill, loyalty, and long-term employment. Even when an employee decides to leave the company, your investment in their personal and business growth will pay dividends in the greater community. This type of stewardship takes a focused effort. Management must think about how to measure the effort and what the outcome looks like.

Stewarding partners may seem a strange concept. I define partners as customers and vendors. Business training would suggest that for a business to succeed, it must squeeze as much money from the customer as possible and pay as little to vendors as they can get away with. Stewardship looks at partners from a different perspective. All sustainable businesses rely on some level of relationship with customers and vendors. Good stewardship then puts a high priority on building relationships. What are the goals and needs of your partners? How can you help them achieve their goals while still being faithful to your stewardship of profits? If you are willing to show a genuine interest in understanding your partners, will you likely build trust, loyalty, and a reciprocating interest? Of course, there will be exceptions, but I advise not to make rules around exceptions but to focus on the good outcomes and how to achieve them.

Finally, stewarding places is not just an environmental concern. Place is the community that your business spends its time in. The community may be other like-minded businesses, employee groups, or the physical community your company does business in. What can you do to help your community flourish? Business is the economic engine of our society, and business owners must take an active role in stewarding that engine so that the community is operating well on all cylinders. Business, civic, education, nonprofit, and faith-based organizations all play a role within our communities. A community will flourish when these sectors work together towards the same goals.

Evidence suggests that businesses should begin looking beyond simply attaining as high of a net profit as possible and look at ways to be part of helping a community flourish. When a company generates a reasonable profit, invests in the people who work for it, is careful not to abuse the environment, and treats customers and vendors respectfully, the community will flourish. These actions create long-term sustainability. Being a good steward of the four Ps will help a business create a positive image with the public and build trust, loyalty, and customers for life.

Generosity to your partners, employees, customers, and communities around you needs to become the new business philosophy. Over the past decade, we systematized everything we do, automated whatever we could, and created a world void of emotions and vested interests. However, the most successful businesses are owned by and employ emotionally invested people. These people care deeply about the company and its role in its growth. They are intensely proud of the business's culture and their impact at every touchpoint and interaction.

A business that focuses on the four principles of stewardship, generosity, and sustainability will succeed. This book dives deep into each principle, providing practical insights into building a culture of stewardship in your business environment.

Chapter 2 – A New Way of Thinking

> *"I alone cannot change the world, but I can cast a stone across the waters to create many ripples." Mother Teresa*
>
> *The greatness of a community is most accurately measured by the compassionate actions of its members. Coretta Scott King*

Building a Culture of Generosity, Collaboration, Community, and Connectedness

In a world grappling with profound social and economic challenges, there is a growing belief that businesses should take the lead in addressing these challenges. This perspective stems from recognizing that companies have significant resources, global influence, and the organizational capacity to effect substantial change.

To tackle the world's most pressing challenges, a collective effort involving all sectors of society, including the business sector, is not just necessary, but empowering. Poverty, inequality, climate change, and health crises are not insurmountable barriers, but opportunities for innovative, large-scale solutions. Large businesses are not just bystanders, but key players in this transformative process, thanks to their resources and agility. Multinational corporations can make an immediate, tangible difference on a global scale through their technological expertise.

Engaging in social and economic problem-solving is not just a moral imperative, but a strategic move for businesses. A strong brand reputation not only fosters consumer loyalty but also attracts and retains top talent seeking to work for socially responsible businesses. Businesses that are proactive in addressing the world's challenges are not just adaptable, but ahead of the curve, gaining a competitive advantage. By making the world a better place, businesses are not just navigating the business environment, but shaping it to their advantage.

Corporate Social Responsibility (CSR) is a new buzzword that aligns with the action of solving social and economic challenges. CSR is more than being philanthropic. It integrates social and environmental concerns into business operations and interactions with stakeholders. This integration helps businesses contribute to sustainable development goals and achieve economic objectives. Companies can create value that extends beyond financial returns to encompass social and environmental benefits by addressing the stewardship of profits, people, partners, and places.

The concept that businesses should look beyond financial returns is controversial among many large and small businesses. Some argue that a company's primary responsibility is to generate profits for its owners or shareholders. Solving societal problems will distract from that mission. Businesses can also wield tremendous power that prevents other societal stakeholders from being part of the solution. Businesses sometimes implement changes selfishly without aligning them with broader societal goals. Businesses' efforts in solutions must be transparent, accountable, and in the community's best interest.

Partnerships between businesses, governments, nonprofits, educational institutions, and faith-based organizations are not just beneficial, but essential, to ensure that business contributions are effective and equitable. Such collaboration provides a framework for leveraging the strengths of each sector to comprehensively address complex challenges. For instance, an I.T. company, the government, and a university could collaborate to bridge the digital divide, while a healthcare company and a nonprofit could work together to bring healthcare to underserved communities. The possibilities are limitless.

As the world grapples with escalating social and economic challenges, there is a compelling argument for businesses to step up and lead the way in addressing these issues. With their vast resources, global reach, and operational capacities, businesses are uniquely positioned to implement transformative solutions. This leadership, when executed with integrity, responsibility, transparency, and meaningful partnerships, is a win-win for both the business and the community.

Large corporations, national governments, international nonprofits, and universities can solve global challenges. What about your local community? The same principles of collaboration, integrity, and transparency can lead to challenges the local community faces. The following fictional story provides a road map on how smaller privately held businesses can work to help a community flourish.

A new business began in a small community in Anywhere, USA, led by entrepreneur Allison. As a small manufacturing business, Allison was committed to a revolutionary approach to business. Under her visionary leadership, this company was not just another startup; it was the embodiment of a new way of thinking in business—one that valued generosity, collaboration, community, and connectedness.

With a small team helping to grow the business, it was clear that Allison fostered a different culture than most businesses. There was a culture of openness and generosity. She encouraged her employees to share ideas freely and collaborate without fear of judgment. This nurturing environment became the bedrock of innovation, where creativity flourished, and groundbreaking products were born.

Allison's vision extended beyond the confines of her business. Collaboration was the company's lifeblood, and Allison actively sought out other local businesses to share resources and expertise. By collaborating with other companies, they tackled complex challenges, proving that business success differed from a zero-sum, win-lose game. The effort was collaborative in nature, where everyone could flourish.

Going beyond the business world, Allison committed time and effort towards community engagement. The company regularly organized volunteer events and encouraged its employees to give back to the community that had supported their startup efforts. Employers allocated specific paid hours for employees to participate in park cleanup, work with students, or serve on local nonprofit boards. Employee volunteerism fostered a sense of community responsibility and strengthened the bonds within the community. Allison and other company employees worked with the local government and churches to address the growing challenge of homelessness. They approached the work collaboratively and engaged the homeless population to help with their needed solutions.

This sense of connectedness was deeply engrained in the company culture and was at the heart of its success in business and the community. Allison invested in team-building activities and personal development programs to ensure that her employees felt valued as workers and individuals. Every employee felt valued and loved. The company radiated a sense of belonging and community, and the impact radiated throughout the community.

This approach had a profound impact. The company's innovative and ethically produced products resonated with consumers who valued social responsibility. Partnerships flourished, and the company earned the community's and its leaders' respect.

Their reputation continued to grow, and other businesses began to take notice. Here was a company that was successful and had an excellent reputation in the community. Allison had many opportunities to share the principles of her success. Soon, many other businesses began embracing generosity, collaboration, community, and connectedness. The business landscape was shaped into a movement that helped the community flourish.

Ultimately, Allison's business became a beacon of hope for a new way of doing business. It built a legacy that lasted well beyond Allison's business ownership. The community realized that a successful business is not just about profits but about creating a better world for everyone.

Today's immense social and economic challenges call for businesses, both large and small, to begin to think and operate in a new and fundamentally different way. Their focus should no longer be solely on profitability and market value. New strategies that address profits, ethics, and socially responsible action must be developed in the business culture. Business plays a central role in our communities, and we must take responsibility for the stewardship of these communities.

Good stewards carefully manage something that belongs to others, such as the community. They must leave the community and the world a better place for future generations.

The social and economic challenges facing society may be too big for any one business or person to respond to and have an impact. How can any business react to the vast wealth gap between the rich and poor, population growth burdening natural resources and food supplies, limited access to clean water, healthcare, and education in developing countries, and social, political, and employment discontent in developed countries? These are massive challenges! They only disappear if businesses and society are willing to think and act differently.

However, economic development comes because business creates opportunities and wealth for many. When enterprises are built on innovation, technology, and entrepreneurial ingenuity, the standard of living will increase. The overall success and economic growth lift, if not all, many boats. And isn't it the government's job to deal with these challenges? Isn't that why businesses and those employed by companies pay taxes? Yes, and yes, that has been, for the most part, true. However, government agencies are reaching their limit, and society is beginning to resist the increasing reach of government.

Investor capitalism is deeply embedded in our society. The concept that the primary objective of business is to increase shareholders' wealth has been the mainstay of business for more than a century. Governments, for the most part, are willing to go along with this idea because they benefit from jobs and taxes. Yet the system itself is creating challenges beyond which the government can deal. Businesses then get increasingly frustrated that the government is wasting tax dollars and not solving the significant issues of the day. Taxes become a burden, and pressure mounts to reduce taxes to a bare minimum. Tax reduction only accelerates the impact of the challenges.

The conversation on shareholder wealth leads us back to the question of stewardship. Whose responsibility is it to steward our communities? Over the past century, only a handful of values-based companies have been able to transfer an attitude of stewardship to the next generation of leaders in the company. Why is embedding stewardship principles into a company so tricky? The widespread belief is that a company can't be profitable and do good in the community. The focus remains on increasing profits and creating more efficient processes. Stewardship is seen as a liability and not an asset. The government then makes laws and policies to favor the shareholder at the expense of the other stakeholders in the business, a vicious cycle that perpetuates itself.

A fundamental shift in business is needed for proper stewardship to impact the lives of families, organizations, and communities that can flourish. This socially responsible behavior is beginning to be demanded by many communities. The belief that appropriate corporate culture is the key to efficiency and sustainability is taking root. This type of culture change includes new ways of organizing, planning, measuring, rewarding, and leading—a new way of thinking. The ultimate goal is to be part of a world where sustainable, effective, and profitable organizations provide sufficient and meaningful employment. Creating innovations that contribute to human development, the quality of life, and a sustainable environment. These fundamentals are the view of the steward of the future.

Since the Industrial Revolution, there have been examples of leaders who have worked towards being a good steward. Interested, you can research and learn more about these leaders.

Robert Owen – Textiles; James Cash (J.C.) Penney – Retail Consumer Goods; William Lever – Soap; James Lincoln – Electric welders; John Spedan Lewis – Clothing; Anita Roddick – Skin Care; Thornton Bradshaw – ARCO; Robert Wood Johnson – Johnson & Johnson.

The key to their success as good stewards is a robust ethical compass, respect for people, and a commitment to their values. If we want more socially responsible companies, we need more value-based leaders willing to create shared value for all stakeholders.

Chapter 3 – Beyond Words: Using Values as a Catalyst for Action

> *"Success seems to be connected to action. Successful people keep moving. They make mistakes but don't quit. Conrad Hilton*

Many businesses list value statements on their websites. The challenge for most companies is to live out those values in the business's day-to-day operations. It is easy to say, "We value integrity" or "Our values are customer centric." However, the reality of living out those intentions needs to be remembered in the rush to build a successful business. In many cases, business leaders have yet to define their values and what they look like in a business context.

Over the course of my career, I followed a set of values but needed more time to write them down and define them. As I began to put words to my understanding of what a noble CFO looks like, I took a closer look at the values that have created a successful career. I knew the technical aspects of being a Controller or CFO. I understood financial reports, cash flow statements, KPIs, and metrics. However, that was not the "secret sauce" of my long-term success as an outsourced CFO. In my book, 'The Noble CFO ', which is a guide to starting and growing a fractional CFO practice, I identified five values as mission-critical to my business success. These five values are foundational to my understanding of stewardship and generosity in business.

1. Develop Authentic Relationships – As humans, we naturally crave connections. When we meet someone new, our brains instinctively search for signs of trustworthiness and authenticity. Building authentic relationships in business is not just a passing trend. These relationships allow people to connect with you and your business on a personal level, leading to more fruitful interactions. Each person gains a deeper understanding of the other, fostering trust and mutual respect.

When you know someone personally, you will better understand what motivates them professionally. You will also encourage your prospects and clients to engage with you and become ambassadors. Personal engagement brings substance to your services, elevating your business above the competition. Your brand is identified as influential, reliable, and trustworthy.

Developing authentic relationships with employees, customers, vendors, and community members sounds like an unattainable goal. Indeed, you will not have to find a way to enter into an authentic relationship with everyone you meet, and you may want to do so. However, being intentional about building relationships and having that value at the forefront of your mind will go a long way toward helping your business thrive.

2. Operate in Integrity—Integrity is the cornerstone of honesty and strong moral principles. Many businesses claim to uphold this value. However, if a company is found to lack integrity, the consequences can be severe. Employees may leave, customers may stop buying, and vendors may avoid you. The community may question your intentions. Upholding integrity is not just a value, it's a necessity for sustainable, long-term business growth and success.

Integrity demands that we do the right thing because it is the right thing to do. Recognized and respected leaders do everything they can to fulfill their promises. Telling the truth is not always the easiest thing to do, but leaders with integrity are fearless in facing the truth. Integrity also means that a leader will acknowledge that they could be wrong. Integrity in business is essential for sustainable, long-term business growth and success. It can be complicated to define and difficult to measure, but you know it when you see it, and it's clear when it's not there.

3. Pursue an Attitude of Service – The qualities associated with strong leadership and sound management in a business seldom include an attitude of service. Executives in a position of power would look at servanthood as a weakness and below their dignity. This thinking would be incorrect. You will learn that pursuing an attitude of service is a characteristic of success for many businesses. They have a people-focused culture that ensures meaningful stability during rapid change. Many business thinkers and writers recognize the value of servant leadership, which is a leadership style that puts others before self. This attitude is increasingly relevant to the challenges in today's business.

As with any theory or philosophy, challenges arise when theory meets practice. In an ideal world, everyone would be eager to serve one another. Those leading would always have the best interests of others in mind, and those being led would willingly submit to any servant leader who steps forward. Institutions would rise with the ethos of servanthood, and Trustees would spend time serving in their capacity because they love the organization and the people they serve. The reality is that we live in a world that is often rife with greed, jealousy, and self-centeredness. Many leaders are corrupted at least partially by power and will usually have a self-advancing agenda as a motive to lead as a servant.

Yet, the principles of servant leadership are valid and should be our expectation of our business leaders. While we cannot control how others lead, we should be willing to set the example of pursuing an attitude of service. There will be times when a servant leader is taken advantage of. But overall, the value is worthy of pursuit, creating a better world.

4. Value the Individual- The fundamental importance of democracy is that every individual matters. No matter what walk of life a person comes from, each opinion and voice is unique. Today's workplace environment has remained relatively the same in the past 250 years. Bureaucratic behavior remains the heart and soul of most work environments, and managers tend to treat workers like children who cannot make good decisions and think for themselves.

A business should treat every individual it interacts with in a way that values their dignity and worth. When a company values the individual employee, the organizational performance and success criteria are not measured primarily financially. Instead, the workplace is filled with joy for the ordinary worker and is measured by the worker's quality of life. Leaders who are passionate about people and value each individual will also find joy at work.

This value plays out with vendors and customers as well. When they understand and feel that they are being treated with dignity and value as individuals by a business, good things will result. Many studies have compared customer acquisition costs to customer retention costs. It is widely accepted that acquiring a new customer costs five times more than retaining an existing customer. Spending time and money, making personal connections to customers, and understanding their needs will be money well spent.

5. Operate in Grace– Grace treats others with respect and dignity in business. Grace encourages business associates and is a source of positive energy. I love the concept of "Grace in Business." It is a beautiful principle! I have worked my whole career with this principle in mind. If I show people they are appreciated, valued, and heard, they inevitably work harder and try to live up to expectations. Extending grace gives the gift of dignity. I treat each person as a person, not an object or "asset." Each person I interact with in business is a person with dreams, feelings, and needs.

Grace allows one to be vulnerable with others, which only deepens trust and relationships. Grace combines many qualities of how one treats or values others. Grace presents itself by showing respect and treating others with dignity. Grace encourages and helps others and creates positive energy with team members. Grace assists others in feeling good about themselves. We all need grace in our lives at some point.

Grace in business can be summed up by the extraordinary stewardship of authentic relationships developed and operating with integrity, an attitude of service, and placing value on the individual.

A Practical Guide to Authentic Relationships

Developing and maintaining authentic relationships takes intentionality and focus. Each point below is relatively easy to do but very easy not to do.

1. Looke to serve before you are served. What can you do to provide value to the other person? Put your own needs and wants on hold as you develop the relationship.

2. Do not allow fear to prevent you from acting. Fear of being taken advantage of or rejected will cause you to miss out on the potential of creating deep relationships.

3. Approach relationships with boldness. Live, speak, and act with courage, passion, and truth.

4. Be your authentic self. This may go without saying, but if you want genuine relationships, you need to be authentic in your passion and mission every moment of the day.

5. Consistency is critical in developing long-term relationships. Trust and understanding naturally develop when a person experiences the consistent message that you care about their well-being.

6. Always be willing to take responsibility for your mistakes. Authenticity means being transparent.

7. Be accountable for your promises. If you tell someone you will do something for them, follow through.

8. Developing authentic relationships takes time and attention. Give your full attention to the people you are talking with. Be willing to share your knowledge and expertise for their benefit and not your own.

The real power of authenticity can be uncomfortable and scary at times. Embracing authentic relationships in business will always inspire others and bring value to all involved. Genuine relationships are the future of business.

A Practical Guide to Developing Integrity

There are several things to keep in mind as you navigate the business world with integrity:

1. An acknowledgment that our laws are based on right and wrong ethics.

2. Industry or company codes of ethics are essential to follow.

3. Almost all humans have a general sense of right and wrong or a moral compass they should follow.

4. Obey the Golden Rule: Do unto others what you would have them do to you.

5. If you don't want the public to see what you are doing, don't do it.

6. Not harm others that people would consider irresponsible.

The following may not seem related to integrity, but I have found that a person of integrity has many of the following characteristics:

1. They are continually learning and working on improving themselves.

2. They are service-oriented, always looking to help others.

3. They radiate positive energy and a can-do attitude

4. They believe in other people and willingly invest themselves in others

5. They lead balanced lives. They realize that there is more to life than just making money.

6. They look at life as an adventure and make the most of it.

Do you see yourself in these characteristics? If not, consider ways to focus on never-ending improvement.

A Practical Guide to Pursuing an Attitude of Service

Pursuing an attitude of service is a characteristic of success for many businesses. They have a people-focused culture that ensures meaningful stability during rapid change. Many business thinkers and writers recognize the value of servant leadership, which is increasingly relevant to the challenges in today's business.

> *"The key to greatness is to look for people's potential and spend time developing it."* Peter Drucker

To help us recognize servant leadership, Robert Greenleaf tested servant leaders in business and servant-leadership organizations. He called it the Best Test:

1. Do those serve to grow as people?

2. While serving, do they become healthier, wiser, more accessible, autonomous, and more likely to become servants?

3. What is the effect on the least privileged in society?

4. Will they benefit or at least not be further deprived?

To be an effective servant leader, you must be honest and accountable for your actions. You should possess a high degree of emotional intelligence. You must be competent for the job at hand. Your attitude must be that of someone willing to learn and coachable. This attitude includes self-awareness about your strengths and weaknesses.

Practical Guide for Valuing Individuals

How do I show my employees I value them?

Give employees the authority and responsibility to make critical decisions directly impacting their work.

Provide guilt-free time off for each employee.

Show that you care by asking questions and getting to know each employee personally.

How do I show my vendors that I value them?

focus on the value the partnership creates for both of you

Do the right thing. No vendor should suffer because of decisions we make

Have ongoing conversations with existing vendors to maintain the relationship

How Do I show my customers that I value them?

Keep your promises.

Could you treat them with respect?

Listen to what they need, not what you want to sell them

Survey your customers to find out how they perceive your company

In the long run, businesses that value the individuals they work with will likely create a flourishing business stronger than businesses that do not value the people they interact with. Hiring and training new employees is expensive. Vendors who are not treated with respect will increase their prices. The cost of finding new customers far outweighs the cost of time to nurture and build long-term relationships with them. The reality? Running a business that respects and values each person is more fun.

A Practical Guide to Operating in Grace

Operating in grace and love in business is not for the faint of heart. The traditional business culture rarely expresses itself in grace and love. If you are inspired to live out grace and love in the workplace, consider the following actions demonstrating grace and love.

- Listen to what others are saying

- Ask engaging questions

- Share information about a project or vision of the company

- Be transparent with your team

- Reframe challenges as learning opportunities

- Support others in their endeavors

- Use humor in a positive way

- Be willing to mentor those not as experienced as yourself

- Engage the opinions of others

- Communicate in a clear and caring way

- Take accountability for your actions and decisions

- Invest in people and cheer on people's personal growth

- Celebrate wins together

We care for people, acknowledge our weaknesses, and treat people with respect and dignity. Is this too much to ask for in business?

Chapter 4 - Business Stewardship: What Does That Really Mean?

> *Stewardship begins with the willingness to be accountable for a larger body than ourselves - an organization, a community. Peter Block*

What is Stewardship?

The term 'stewardship' holds significant relevance in the business context. It encompasses the conduct, supervision, or management of something, particularly the careful and responsible management of something entrusted to one's care.

Stewardship is about service to something greater. It asks us to be deeply accountable for our organizations' outcomes without trying to control others or take care of them. It requires redistributing power and privilege, moving choice and resources closer to the organization's edges.

Peter Block's book *Stewardship: Choosing Service over Self-Interest* approaches the issue of leadership in the face of the changing business environment from a stewardship perspective. His primary thesis is that the focus on individual leaders as the critical agents for meeting the new marketplace's challenges is misplaced. Instead, he believes that "it is this pervasive and almost religious belief in leaders that slows the process of genuine reform." On the other hand, empowerment is the belief that the answer to many problematic business questions lies within each person working for an organization. Stewardship then becomes an issue of giving away power to those who may have the most minor "important" position in a company to make decisions. Block drives to the heart of the issue by saying:

Stewardship begins with the willingness to be accountable for a larger body than ourselves—an organization or a community. It springs from a set of beliefs about reforming organizations that affirms our choice for service over the pursuit of self-interest. When we choose service over self-interest, we say we are willing to be deeply accountable without controlling the world around us.

Stewardship: A Deeper Look

Service over self-interest is entirely counter to how most business leaders have been trained. The idea that leaders would willingly put themselves in a position requiring them to be held accountable for an action or decision entirely outside of their control is unlikely. And yet, this is a critical part of creating an environment of extraordinary business stewardship. Trusting and believing in every person's decision-making ability, regardless of their position, lays the foundation for a transformational stewardship environment, making everyone feel valued and trusted.

The business world has focused much of its time and resources on developing a monetary return on investment as possible. As a result, shareholders and executive leadership of large publicly held businesses have experienced incredible growth in wealth over the past few decades. However, this single focus on monetary return has produced an ever-growing culture of greed and malfeasance with the likes of Enron, WorldCom, Tyco, Global Crossing, Wells Fargo, Volkswagen, Valeant Pharmaceutical, etc.

Simultaneous with this growth in wealth, the income or wealth gap continues to grow, with most of the nation's wealth under the control of those responsible for leading businesses. Before President Obama's 2014 State of the Union Address, the media reported that the top wealthiest 1 percent possess 40 percent of the nation's wealth; the bottom 80 percent own 7 percent. The media recently reported that the "richest 1 percent in the United States now own more additional income than the bottom 90 percent." The gap between the top 10 percent and the middle class is over 1,000 percent; that increases another 1,000 percent for the top 1 percent. The average employee "needs to work more than a month to earn what the CEO makes in one hour."

The traditional business approach often revolves around scale and speed, cost reduction, and outperforming competitors. It's frequently viewed as a zero-sum game, where one party's gain is another's loss. However, there's a need to consider a win-win environment. While the concept of win-lose may hold true in gambling, in business, the focus should be on creating an environment where a company can be profitable, people can be developed, partners can be treated fairly, and the community can thrive.

Corporate and small businesses in America should begin looking beyond attaining as high a net profit as possible. They should start seeking ways to help their people develop to their best potential, operating with integrity and fairness with vendors and customers, and working towards helping their communities flourish. By adopting the stewardship approach, businesses can make a significant positive impact on the community, fostering a sense of responsibility and commitment. This is a company that generates a reasonable profit, develops the people who work for it, treats clients and vendors respectfully, and proactively invests in the community.

A Story of Stewardship

COVID-19 has created multiple challenges for businesses and our economy in general. When the order to shut down non-essential companies came down from the Governor of Washington, there was a scramble to figure out what businesses were essential. Most of my clients were deemed essential services and continued to operate. However, that did not ease the anxiety about how a collapsing economy would affect business. When the federal government introduced the Paycheck Protection Program (PPP) through the SBA, there was an overall sense of relief to have a source of funds if the virus and economy worsened.

A1 Pallets was one such company. We determined it was an essential business because it supplied pallets to the primary transportation industry. Amrik's business has grown steadily over the past few years and has produced a substantial cash balance. The company also incurred debt for automating the pallet manufacturing process. Business remained strong as the pandemic spread throughout the country. A1 Pallets would come out relatively unscathed through this national emergency.

The decision to apply for the PPP loan was made as the cash balance remained steady, revenue remained constant, and the business's future was strong. Should we apply for the loan? We were relatively confident we could have the entire loan forgiven through the forgiveness program, so this was, in essence, "free" money. Could we argue that we were sufficiently concerned about how COVID-19 might impact the company? We decided that we met the qualifications for the loan and proceeded to fill out the applications. Amrik's enterprise comprises three businesses with employees, so applications were submitted to all three firms.

The question may come to the reader's mind regarding how this relates to stewardship. As I was advising Amrik about the PPP loan, I was filtering my advice through the lens of stewardship. First, there was no guarantee that the virus would not impact the business in the future. If the economy turned into a recession due to the virus, building additional reserves to face a potentially severe recession would be prudent and sound stewardship. Second, we qualified for the loans, and it was reasonable to take advantage of a government program that we qualified for and would ensure that personnel pay would be maintained. Third, I told Amrik that if, at the end of the virus and the lingering effects, it was clear that we did not need the extra funds, he should consider contributing them to his family foundation. This foundation was started to help fund a hospital building in the small village in India where Amrik grew up.

After filtering the decision through the matrix of stewarding profits, people, partners, and places, it became easy to make a decision that matched my values well.

Evidence of Stewardship

Many of us are familiar with "the triple bottom line." This phrase was first coined in 1994 by John Elkington, the founder of a British consultancy called SustainAbility. He argued that companies should prepare three different (entirely separate) bottom lines. The triple bottom line (TBL) consists of three Ps: profit, people, and the planet. I would add a fourth P for partners, representing customers and vendors. TBL aims to measure the corporation's financial, social, and environmental performance over a set period. In the view of many, focusing attention on all three of these areas creates a sustainable business: a company that makes profits for its shareholders while protecting the environment and improving the lives of those with whom it interacts. It operates in such a way that business, environmental, and societal interests all intersect.

The foundation for building a sustainable business is to make a profit. But how much profit is necessary to sustain a business? How much of that profit should be invested back into the business? How much should go into the business owner's pocket? Good profit stewardship carefully plans the answer to each of these questions. The long-term sustainability of the business depends on achieving the proper balance of stewarding the business's earnings.

I'm frequently called to resolve a crisis caused by low-growth planning. Business explodes, yet industry needs more cash reserves. There's a demand for their product; however, the cash bottleneck kills the company before selling it. A business needs to steward profits and cash, so the cash shortages that growth often produces are built into its expansion strategy. Business growth is usually a challenging ride. There are ups and downs, growth, and slowing. Stewardship demands that cash flow pinches are recognized and planned for.

A primary factor in most businesses' success is those working for the company. Caring for the people who work for the industry by investing in their education, training, compensation, motivation, and empowerment creates a culture and environment in which people want to give their best to the company with long-term employment. Stewarding people is a formula to create the environment that allows a company to flourish.

A good steward of people in business recognizes the importance of encouraging time off for employees. They realize that creating an environment of work-life balance increases productivity and creativity. This begins with the leader's attitude toward maintaining balance in life. The swells of failing to prioritize relationships and health will affect business—often negatively. Karen Sumberg, vice president and director of projects and communications at the Center for Work-Life

Policy, says, "You get tremendous burnout where people are not working at their full potential, they're not excited anymore, they're just perpetually tired." That's not good for business.

Traditional business training suggests that a successful business is built by getting the most money from the customer and paying the least to the vendors. Stewarding partners would mean understanding the value of building loyalty with your customers and vendors by helping them flourish.

Stewarding your customers means not charging the maximum price or giving extended credit terms. Invest in developing expertise. Your customer's perception of superior customer service is best understood when you take the time to know your customer. Excellent customer service springs from a foundation of truly understanding your product or service and your customer. Using this knowledge to craft an experience for your customer that's targeted and feels personal is an investment toward achieving recognition for incredibly excellent customer service.

For the vendor, it may mean paying the bill faster than when it is due or not buying from the cheapest supplier. When a vendor relationship begins, it is easy to focus on what the vendor will do for you. However, partnerships will fail to form if the ongoing connection is only about you. Without the sense that you have a vested interest in their success, most vendors do the expected. Nothing motivates them to look for exceptional ways to help your business. Become a value creator. Becoming a successful steward of partners begins with you. Building loyalty through stewardship is an excellent insurance policy.

Every business is part of the community that surrounds it. In many ways, it is the community that supports the business endeavor. A business needs to steward this relationship with the community in a way that allows the community to flourish. Healthy communities foster a healthy business environment. Small businesses need to work in partnership with each other and their community to gain an economy of scale and influence to compete with more giant corporations. There is power in unity and the collective efforts of business and community. When stewardship of place focuses on the business community, so much more can be accomplished in the community. Supporting the community's civic, educational, nonprofit, and faith sectors is also suitable for business.

Application

Stewardship is all great in theory, but what are some practical ways a business owner or leader can implement this strategy? How can a traditional numbers CFO start looking at business as a CSO (Chief Stewardship Officer)?

1. Stewarding profits means identifying what net profit is adequate to provide a reasonable return for the owner's investment and not distributing more than this amount to the owner.

2. Stewarding profits means determining how much working capital is necessary for a business to operate safely and investing the rest in personnel and the community.

3. Stewarding people means treating personnel as partners in the business and not as a resource or asset.

4. Stewarding people means investing in personnel to help them become better workers, parents, spouses, and community leaders.

5. Stewarding partners means helping customers and vendors become successful in their businesses.

6. Stewarding partners means developing relationships with customers and vendors and understanding what is important to them.

7. Stewarding places means investing in the community in ways that allow the community to flourish.

8. Stewarding places means understanding the community is as crucial to your business success as you are.

Chapter 5 - Stewarding Profits

> *"Profit for a company is like oxygen for a person. If you don't have enough of it, you're out of the game. But if you think your life is about breathing, you're really missing something."*
> *Peter Drucker*

How Much is Enough?

Economic insatiability is rooted in human nature. It is in our nature to compare our fortune with our fellow humans and find it wanting. Capitalism has dramatically intensified this insatiability, making it the psychological basis of an entire civilization and now commonplace in everyday life.

Imagine a world in which most people worked only fifteen hours a week. They would be paid as much as, or even more than, they now are because the fruits of their labor would be distributed more evenly across society. Leisure would occupy far more of their waking hours than work. Maynard Keynes proposed this idea in 1930 in a published essay *"Economic Possibilities for Our Grandchildren"*.

His thesis was straightforward. As technological progress increased the output of goods per hour worked, people would have to work less and less to satisfy their needs until, in the end, they would not have to work hard at all.

This essay's first question is, "What is wealth for?" For well-balanced individuals and healthy communities, making money cannot be an end in of itself. At no level of material wealth will I feel satisfied with what I have because someone will always do more than I do? Once the competition for wealth turns into a competition for status, it becomes a zero-sum game because everyone, by definition, cannot have high status. As the late H. L. Hunt, then one of the wealthiest men in the world, put it, money is "just a way of keeping score."

The American combination of social equality and income inequality has since become the capitalist norm, leading to a situation in which every member of society competes against each other. And the greater the disparity, the greater the competitive pressure. The coexistence of great wealth and poverty, especially in societies with enough for everyone, should offend our sense of justice. What would that look like if we could imagine that everyone has enough to lead a good life?

The aim of policy and other forms of collective action should be to secure an economic organization that puts the good things of life – health, respect, friendship, leisure, etc. – within reach of all.

Why Values in Stewardship Matter

The business world has focused much of its time and resources on developing a significant monetary return on investment. As a result, shareholders and executive leadership of large publicly held businesses have experienced incredible wealth growth over the past few decades.

Formal business education and practice focus on bringing the maximum return on shareholders' and business owners' investments. The myth is that profit is the ultimate purpose of owning a business. Profit or loss is simply an outcome of operating a business. History has shown us many examples of companies that operated solely to maximize profits, got caught up in scandals, and compromised business decisions. You get the picture: Standard Oil, TWA, Enron, Lincoln Savings & Loan, E.F. Hutton, Arthur Andersen, WorldCom, Tyco International, Bear Stearns, and Lehman Brothers. The list of CFOs who have gone to jail because they either had no values or compromised to meet the increasing profit demand is also long. Most of the companies listed above had their finance chiefs go to jail. Profit should never trump values in the business world.

Unfortunately, the companies that spectacularly fail because of corruption and a sole focus on profits make the headlines. What about business success stories? These stories may be harder to find, but they are out there. In his books *Good To Great* and *Built to Last*, Jim Collins describes several businesses that operated on a values-based premise. Costco has been a phenomenal success as well. They are profitable, their employees are loyal, and their customers love them. Costco had four values, which they called a code of ethics. 1) obey the law, 2) take care of our members, 3) take care of our employees, and 4) respect our vendors. These values set the foundation for a successful, well-loved business. Jim Sinegal, the founder of Costco, said, "Culture isn't the most important thing; it's the only thing." Zappos is another wildly successful company and built its success on ten core values. The values are personal, meaningful, and unique to that business. The values tell you what this business stands for. As noted earlier in this chapter, Gravity Payments had core values that reflected the service and value of the individual. Dan Price valued his employees and believed every employee should make a livable wage. He has doubled his revenue and profit.

The evidence is clear for these companies that having core values as the foundation of the business drives them to success. A written and communicated set of core values enables employees to make decisions that benefit the company with onerous oversight. These values must be lived out in the company culture throughout the organization. If the leaders do not follow the values, the rest of the employees will not follow the values, and the customers will sense the dissonance between words and actions. Today's entrepreneurs are changing the business world. Innovation and solutions built on values are the future of business. Companies that stand on values today will be the business leaders of tomorrow.

Entrepreneurs and business owners want to build a sustainable business. The critical piece of building a long-term sustainable business is to lay a foundation of core values from which to operate. Here are some simple points to consider when accomplishing this objective.

Identify your core values – This would appear to be an obvious suggestion. Still, many people have not gone through the exercise of understanding and writing down what is most important to them. Consider how you have responded to people and actions in the past. What has caused you to say that this is what I believe in or an area I will not tolerate? Write out your thoughts and hone them into several essential values in your life.

Define your values. When you say integrity is a core value, what does that mean for you? Provide some narrative around the definition of a particular core value. Words have different meanings to different people depending on their context.

Write out examples of how your core values are lived out in your life. It will be easier for others to understand your core values when you show examples of how you live them.

Align yourself with other individuals who reflect your values. Partnerships and collaborations are strong. Finding the people you align with will make your journey to follow your values much more accessible.

Communicate your values with clarity. Once you have decided on what values are important to you, take the opportunity to share these values with others. The more people understand who you are and what you stand for, the more likely they will support and do business with you.

Attract others to your core values. When prospecting for new clients or networking with business associates, wear your values on your sleeve. Keep the opportunity from passing by sharing your values in some way.

Open yourself to accountability. The more you share and live your values, the more people will expect to see them in your life. Being consistent in living out your values will reinforce their importance.

A Practical Guide to Stewarding Profits

The foundation for building a sustainable business is to make a profit. But how much profit is necessary to sustain a business? How much of that profit should be invested back into the business? How much should go into the business owner's pocket? Good profit stewardship carefully plans the answer to each of these questions. The long-term sustainability of the business depends on achieving the proper balance of stewarding the business's earnings.

I'm frequently called in to resolve a crisis caused by low-growth planning. Business explodes, yet the business needs more cash reserves. There's a demand for their product; however, the cash bottleneck kills the company before selling it. A business needs to steward profits and cash, so the cash shortages that growth often produces are built into its expansion strategy. Business growth is usually a challenging ride. There are ups and downs, growth, and slowing. Stewardship demands that cash flow pinches are recognized and planned for.

Helping business owners understand "how much is enough" in their business involves helping them establish clear goals, understand their financial health, recognize the balance between growth and sustainability, and appreciate their business's non-financial aspects. Here are ten main points to focus on.

Defining Business Goals and Success Metrics: Every business owner should clearly understand what success looks like for their business. This involves setting specific, measurable goals related to revenue, profit, market share, customer satisfaction, etc. The business owner should consider both short-term and long-term objectives for their business,

Financial Health and Metrics: Business owners must understand vital financial metrics such as revenue, profit margins, cash flow, and return on investment (ROI). They should know how to read financial statements like balance sheets, income statements, and cash flow statements to gauge the health of their business.

Understanding Market and Industry Standards: Comparing the business's performance against industry benchmarks can help owners know where they stand. This includes understanding the industry's average profit margins, growth rates, and key performance indicators (KPIs).

Cost Management and Efficiency: A business owner should be educated on identifying and controlling operational costs and investing in areas that yield the highest return. This also involves understanding the difference between essential costs and discretionary spending.

Growth vs. Sustainability: A business owner must understand how to balance development with sustainability. Rapid growth can lead to challenges such as overexpansion, quality control issues, or cash flow problems. Sustainable growth focuses on long-term stability.

Personal Financial Goals: Business owners must align their financial goals with business performance. This includes understanding how much they need to draw from the business for personal expenses, retirement plans, and other personal financial objectives.

Work-Life Balance: Many business owners work long hours each day and often work on weekends. They believe that the more involved they are in the day-to-day operations, the more successful the business will be. This does not have to be the case. Success isn't only measured financially; it includes quality of life and personal satisfaction. Steward profits in a way that allows the business owner to hire people as good as or better at running the business's operations.

Social and Ethical Responsibility: The business owner must consider the broader impact of their business on the community. They should always run an ethical company, considering how their actions impact others and the environment.

Exit Strategy and Succession Planning: A business owner will not live forever! They must plan for the future, including potential exit strategies. The succession plan may include the next generation, employee ownership, or another business with similar values. The long-term vision for the company should consist of exiting the industry with the most negligible impact on the employees and community.

Continual Learning and Adaptability: In a constantly changing business environment, the business owner should be committed to learning and adapting to new trends, technologies, and market shifts. Resources should be available to adapt to changes.

As you can see, "how much is enough" encompasses various areas beyond finances.

Chapter 6 – Stewarding People

> *"When people are financially invested, they want a return. When people are emotionally invested, they want to contribute." Simon Sinek*

Why each employee matters to business success

The Industrial Revolution, a pivotal period in history, revolutionized production and distribution in business, setting the stage for modern workplaces. However, despite the significant changes in technology and society, our work environments have remained largely unchanged for the past 250 years. The Industrial Revolution's profound influence on companies and organizations has led to a reluctance to deviate from past success. Bureaucratic behavior, a relic of the past, still dominates most work environments, with managers often adopting a paternalistic approach toward their employees. The prevailing belief is that the higher the management level, the better the decisions.

Traditionally, employee engagement has been driven by external motivators, often referred to as the 'carrot-and-stick' approach. This approach, rooted in the belief that humans respond to rewards and punishments, has been a cornerstone of business management.

However, history has shown that this approach is not always effective in the long run and can even be counterproductive. A paradigm shift is needed, one that recognizes the power of intrinsic motivation.

The success of most businesses hinges on the people who work for them. Investing in the education, training, compensation, motivation, and empowerment of these individuals is not just a sound business strategy, but also a way to foster a culture of commitment and loyalty. Stewarding people is not just about managing them, but about creating an environment where they can thrive and contribute their best to the company over the long term. It is a formula for a company's success.

Stewarding people should result in a work environment that is both fun and fulfilling. The average worker worldwide finds fulfillment and joy when their ability to make essential and critical business decisions is recognized. The worker whose job is most impacted by a decision should make the decision. This decision's critical component must include input from coworkers and supervisors. If input is received and relied on, it doesn't matter if the decision is good or bad. Everyone makes mistakes occasionally. These are critical learning times for employees, which only strengthen the ability of each worker to make better decisions.

Daniel Pink's book *Drive* expands on the research of behavioral scientists of the last few decades who have discovered a different human drive. In the past, motivation has been fueled more by extrinsic desires than intrinsic ones. Motivational behavior was concerned more with external rewards to which an activity leads rather than the inherent satisfaction of the activity itself.

Daniel Pink suggests that business today needs to take a different approach. This new approach has three essential elements: Autonomy, Mastery, and Purpose.

1. Give Employees Autonomy

By nature, humans want to be "autonomous and self-directed." Pink suggests empowering employees to explore new ideas, allowing them to work flexible schedules, giving them a say in hiring new talent, and letting them decide how to tackle a problem. This not only fosters a sense of ownership but also opens doors for personal growth and development, inspiring them to reach their full potential.

2. Give Employees Mastery Opportunities.

Pink says, "Making progress in one's work is the most motivating aspect of many jobs." You can help employees progress by working closely with them to assign tasks matching their skill levels so employees are neither anxious nor bored.

3. Give Employees a Sense of Purpose.

"Humans, by their nature, seek purpose—to make a contribution and be a part of a cause greater and more enduring than themselves," says Pink. You can fulfill your employees' sense of purpose by making community service part of your corporate culture. Try organizing in-office food drives or inviting the team to spend a day volunteering.

If business owners understand and can tap into this new motivational drive, it will strengthen our companies, elevate our lives, and improve the world.

Practical Guide to Stewarding People

If you are a Type-A businessperson, the thought of taking a vacation from work is fraught with questions. Will the company face a crisis while I'm gone? Will anyone care to keep things going at peak efficiency if I need to be there to ensure it happens? Should I wait until the company is stronger financially before I leave?

Your employees may face the same concerns, especially if you have hired motivated employees who thrive on success. They may embrace your drive to keep the company strong and fear that stepping away from their responsibilities could hurt the business.

As a good steward of people in your business, it is your job to create an environment where your employees recognize the importance of vacations. Creating a healthy environment begins with your attitude toward maintaining balance. It may feel like your business is your life. However, relationships and health can only be addressed when you reap a breakdown in these areas. The swells of failing to prioritize relationships and health affect your business—often negatively. By prioritizing a healthy work-life balance through a well-structured vacation policy, you show your employees that their well-being is valued and cared for.

Lead by example. If you must, carry your smartphone and check in once daily. Otherwise, get away from the building that houses your business. Connect in the present with the people that matter the most to you. Unique ideas often materialize when you place yourself in a different environment.

Your Vacation Policy Is Important!

Idea generation also happens when employees step away from their day-to-day work environment. Vacation time rejuvenates, especially when employees enjoy their jobs—even employees who are ambivalent about their work return from vacation with a more positive attitude.

One of the first steps to eliminating the fear that vacation requests may be unwelcome is to create a clear vacation policy. It's common to offer two weeks after the first year, three weeks after two years, and four weeks after more years with the company.

Incorporating personal time off/sick leave days into the company policy is common sense. Who wants their employees to share the latest bug with their coworkers, especially when it could be severe, such as SARS or avian flu? With personal time benefits, this type of vacation policy acknowledges your employees' needs to take a break—spend time with family, travel, tackle a personal project—and do something where the boss doesn't have a say in the outcome.

Whether employees are salaried or receive overtime pay, they can only function at peak without serious time off. Karen Sumberg, vice president and director of projects and communications at the Center for Work-Life Policy, says, "You get tremendous burnout where people are not working at their full potential. They're not excited anymore; they're just perpetually tired." That's not good for business.

Consider Alternative Vacation Policies

Then there's the problem every employer dreams of. If you have a team that cares about the business's success, they may not take their vacations. Penny Herscher, CEO of FirstRain, found "that her long-time employees took less and less vacation time." She didn't believe they were afraid to take a vacation. They were dedicated to their jobs. So, she implemented a new vacation policy—take as much time as you need. This innovative approach encouraged her employees to take much-needed breaks and sparked a sense of excitement and hope for a more balanced and productive work environment.

Herscher believes the policy will keep the amount of vacation time her people take. What "it will change [is] "the level of freedom that our employees feel. If somebody needs to take five weeks, I trust they're making a good decision." This type of vacation policy has business benefits as well. Companies no longer have to track used and unused vacation time or pay employees for unused vacation.

Say "Yes" as often as possible.

If you've made good hiring decisions, your employee's code of ethics will produce some level of internal guilt—especially if you're the type who is always running full out. But if you're always saying, "No, that's not a good time for us," you'll make your best employees feel guilty that they want to take some vacation time.

Most people don't enjoy living with guilt. Eventually, your employees have to evade it. Guilt manifests itself in increased sick days and reduced productivity. It could even result in the employee leaving the company—not always on pleasant terms.

Circumvent this. If you find yourself routinely stacking the schedule with stressful deadlines, start saying "Yes" to vacation requests instead. Give them the dates they request unless there's a good reason to ask your employees not to take certain days off—an industry-wide trade show, a scheduled product launch deadline, or something significant. You'll see positive results. Employees who are well-rested and happy, who have their work lives balanced with their off-work lives, are best positioned to be your most effective and high-performing employees.

Your employees not only deserve time off from work. They need time off. When you clarify, you understand that it reduces distrust and increases loyalty. These are just two benefits of good vacation stewardship.

Six Points to Consider

1. Effective Communication: Clear, honest, and consistent communication with employees is essential. You should encourage open dialogue, listen to employee feedback, and convey expectations and goals.

2. Leadership and Leading by Example: Business owners should lead by example to inspire and motivate their teams. Their behavior sets the tone for the company culture and work ethic. Leadership involves more than management; it's about guiding, inspiring, and supporting the team.

3. Employee Development and Recognition: Investing in employee growth through training and development opportunities is essential. Even if an employee leaves, the business owner who invested in that employee has benefited the greater community. Recognition of good performance will boost morale and loyalty. Recognition can be both monetary and non-monetary.

4. Create a Positive Work Environment: A respectful, inclusive, and supportive work environment enhances employee satisfaction and productivity. The company's culture should value the employee's well-being.

5. Fair and Transparent Policies: It is essential to ensure that all company policies on employment, promotions, and benefits are fair, transparent, and consistently applied. Transparency includes understanding and complying with legal labor standards and creating a workplace where all employees feel valued and treated fairly.

6. Employee Empowerment: This is a repeat of the above. Empower employees by giving them autonomy and responsibility. Empowerment means trusting employees to make decisions, solve problems, and have a say in matters that affect their work.

Following these guidelines will provide a strong foundation for business owners to manage and steward their employees effectively, leading to a more engaged and productive workforce.

Chapter 7 - Stewarding Partners

> *"When clients and vendors work together harmoniously, they create a synergy that benefits both sides. It's not just about the transactions; it's about building lasting partnerships." Stephen Covey*

Create a win-win with clients and vendors

Traditional business training suggests that a successful business is built by getting the most money from the customer and paying the least to the vendors. However, 'stewarding partner' is a different approach that brings mutual benefits. In this context, 'stewarding partner' refers to a business strategy that prioritizes the well-being and success of both customers and vendors. It's about understanding the value of building loyalty with your customers and vendors by helping them flourish, which, in turn, helps your business thrive.

Stewarding your customers is about more than just the price or credit terms. It's about investing in developing expertise and understanding your customers personally. For instance, you can conduct customer surveys to gather feedback and understand their needs better. You can also invest in training your staff to provide excellent customer service. When you truly understand your product or service and your customer, you can craft a personal and targeted experience. This investment in understanding and personalization leads to recognition for incredibly excellent customer service.

Stewarding your vendors is about more than just paying the bill on time. It's about not always choosing the cheapest supplier and considering the long-term benefits of the relationship. When a vendor relationship begins, it's easy to focus on what the vendor will do for you. However, true partnerships are built on mutual trust and fairness. Without the sense that you have a vested interest in their success, most vendors do the expected. Nothing motivates them to look for exceptional ways to help your business. You, as a small business owner, have the power to build solid and sustainable partnerships by becoming a value creator and fostering fairness.

The following fictional story gives insight into how effective stewardship of partners can be.

In a small coastal town, there was a family-owned seafood restaurant named Ocean's Bounty. The owner, Mark, had inherited the business from his father, and he was determined to continue its legacy. Mark's vision for the company differed from the traditional MBA business training he had received. He believed in stewarding partners, customers, and vendors by helping them flourish alongside his business.

Mark started to re-evaluate his pricing strategy. Instead of setting his menu prices based simply on the maximum he could comfortably charge and not lose customers, he decided to look deeper into the quality of the ingredients and the culinary experience his customers would experience. It was important to Mark to make sure each customer felt like the overall experience matched the price. Seldom were his customers disappointed.

Mark wanted to reward his regular customers, so he established a loyalty program. Rewards included special discounts and the opportunity to join a free online community to share ideas about improving the restaurant's experience. Because of the established online community, many customers began recognizing each other when eating at the restaurant. It soon became known as the restaurant to go to for a community experience.

The commercial fishing industry, known for its volatility and fluctuating prices, has had several ups and downs over the years. Mark, as a responsible business owner, wanted to do his part in supporting the local fishermen and suppliers. In the restaurant industry, an owner often finds the freshest and highest quality products for a higher price or finds a mass distributor with lower prices but not as good of quality. Mark decided that to give his customers the best experience, he needed to get the best quality products. He started working with the local suppliers and committed to purchasing locally. He chose to work with local fishermen and suppliers who shared his commitment to sustainability and quality, even if it meant paying a slightly higher price.

With his commitment to the local industry, Mark also knew there would be times when his suppliers would need more cash. Mark always paid his bills promptly and even, at times, paid invoices early to help the local suppliers during these times. This support built trust among his suppliers, and they always gave Mark the best price they could, based on the local fresh market.

Mark's business continued to grow and became a well-known restaurant in the area. However, the stewardship approach came with its challenges. For instance, sometimes, the profit margins were razor-thin, and Mark needed help to be profitable. He thought of finding cheaper suppliers from outside the area or raising menu prices above what he thought was fair. These were tough decisions that tested his commitment to the stewardship approach. Mark stayed on the course because he focused on the long-term health of his relationships with customers and vendors. He believed that this strategy would lead to a more sustainable and successful business in the long term.

Mark's commitment to stewardship began to pay off in unexpected ways. Ocean's Bounty had a fantastic ocean view that attracted many patrons both near and far. That beauty came with risks, and one powerful storm damaged his restaurant extensively. Several of his loyal customers organized a fundraiser to help with repairs. His vendors offered flexible payment terms and ensured deliveries were expedited to help with a rapid reopening. This outpouring of support was a testament to the loyalty Mark had cultivated through his stewardship approach to business. It also demonstrated the resilience and strength of the relationships he had built, which ultimately helped him overcome a challenging situation.

As Ocean's Bounty recovered and continued to thrive, Mark's philosophy of building loyalty through stewardship became a core part of its identity. The restaurant was not just a place to eat but became a community hub where customers and vendors felt valued and respected. Mark's approach demonstrated that business success is more than just the bottom line. Business should be about fostering relationships and creating a mutual support network, where everyone feels a sense of belonging and community.

Stewardship is more than a moral choice but also a strategic choice. By prioritizing the well-being of customers and vendors, businesses can build a foundation of loyalty and trust that can weather any storm and lead to long-term success. As a business owner, your role in this process is crucial. Your decisions and actions directly impact the success of your stewardship approach, making you an integral part of the process.

As a business owner, I know you think about more than the revenue you generate. You also consider the costs your decisions will incur and the resulting margin you retain. Have you ever considered that the vendors you work with also have these concerns? To build winning vendor relationships, it pays to communicate powerfully that you want to partner with your vendors. This can be done by regularly engaging in open and honest communication, showing appreciation for their work, and being transparent about your business goals and challenges. The message should be, 'I want to help you grow and build a successful business as I grow mine.' Do you want your clients to see you as a value creator? Consider the exponential value to you as a business if your vendors also saw you in that light.

Focus on Being a Good Fit

Creating a vision of the potential within each partnership begins with ensuring you're as good a fit for your vendor as they are for you. Recognize the value of your vendor's time, especially when offering a service. Do your research to have a 'lucid understanding 'or a clear and comprehensive understanding of your needs. Then, voice them clearly so your vendors know whether working with you will grow and build their businesses. This clear communication and mutual understanding are key to building strong and successful business relationships.

Also, take some time to get to know your vendor's needs. What motivates their investment in their business? As you do this, you'll identify partners who share complementary business philosophies. This alignment complements your partnering fit.

Exchange Knowledge with Your Vendors

Change Factory, an Australian change management company, says it well. "Vendors hold a wealth of knowledge relating to their products or services. A vendor also holds knowledge of utilization within the industry. That knowledge helps you, as a client, achieve your objectives."

Renate Cunneen suggests in her Huffington Post blog that "the biggest mistake clients make when dealing with outsourced vendors" is to bring vendors on board and then to "not listen to them when they try to give us clear feedback on our shop[.] Part of the growth in human beings and business is listening to what you may be missing in yourself that someone else can see from the outside. Growth is hearing what we don't want to hear, accepting it, facing it, and making the real attempts [sic] to change it. Maybe there are cracks in your business that the vendor can see from the outside; why wouldn't you want this type of feedback? Above all, how many vendors will give you this feedback? Many won't if there is no trust where they feel comfortable enough to share candid feedback. That in itself is a tragedy."

Treat Them as Valued Partners

You'll build a few winning partnerships if you constantly ask, "What's the bottom price you can offer me?" Your message is, "I only care about the value you create for me." Instead, focus on the value the partnership creates for both of you. Louis Grasmick, founder of Louis J. Grasmick Lumber Co., tells the story of a supplier stuck with two boxcars of lumber in transit from the west coast to the eastern seaboard. Their customer had canceled mid-country. While the company still lost money on the deal, Grasmick's willingness to take the loads and sell them at no cost to the supplier became a winning deal for his business. Because Grasmick put himself in the supplier's position and did what he could to reduce the impact of the canceled order, it led to many future profitable arrangements for both Grasmick Lumber and the supplier.

Did Grasmick know this would help his business? No. However, his business embraces two attitudes. 1) "We wouldn't expect anyone to suffer because of us." 2) "It's also important to do the right thing." As a result, he believes their company benefits from advantageous pricing their suppliers don't offer to competitors. Don't slip into the assumption that once you've chosen a vendor, your contribution to the partnership will be completed. Your vendor may know precisely what needs to be done; however, you need ongoing communication to determine the specifics for a winning relationship with your company. Recognize that vendors must return the work to you when seeking more information. They're doing what's necessary to provide the service or quality of materials you hired them to deliver.

When a vendor relationship begins, it's easy to focus on what the vendor will do for you—expectations, etc. However, partnerships will fail to form if the ongoing connection is only about you. Without the sense that you are vested in their success, most vendors do what is expected. Nothing motivates them to look for exceptional ways to help your business. Become a value creator. Becoming a successful partner begins with you.

Five Key Takeaways

1. Understanding and Meeting Needs: Encourage business owners to deeply understand customers' and vendors' needs and expectations. This involves active listening and empathy. For customers, it means providing products or services that meet their needs. For vendors, it means understanding their operational constraints and expectations.

2. Transparent Communication: Promote open and honest communication. This includes transparency about both sides' capabilities, limitations, and expectations. Transparency builds trust, a key ingredient in any win/win relationship.

3. Value Exchange and Fairness: This doesn't necessarily mean the lowest price for customers or the highest profit margin from vendors. Instead, it is a fair trade in which both parties feel they are getting good value.

4. Long-Term Relationships Over Short-Term Gains: Business owners should strive to build lasting and mutually beneficial relationships over time rather than focusing on immediate profits or savings.

5. Flexibility and Adaptability: A business owner should always consider any negations with flexibility in mind. Being willing to adapt to the needs and circumstances of customers and vendors can lead to better outcomes for all parties involved. It may mean customizing services or products for customers or adjusting order terms for vendors.

By focusing on these critical points, business owners can build strong, lasting, mutually beneficial relationships with customers and vendors, leading to a healthier, more sustainable business environment.

Chapter 8 - Stewarding Places

> *"True community requires commitment and openness. It is a willingness to extend yourself to encounter and know the other." David Spangler*

What Does Community Engagement Look Like?

Every business is part of the community that surrounds it. In many ways, the community supports the business endeavor. A company needs to steward this relationship with the community in a way that allows the community to flourish. Healthy communities create a healthy business environment. Supporting the community's civic, education, nonprofit, and faith sectors is good business.

B Lab began in 2006 with the idea that businesses could lead toward a new, stakeholder-driven model. For the past 15 years, B Lab has expressed its values and worked toward serving business leaders in the following ways.

1. Business must be the change that we seek in the world.

2. All business should be conducted as if people and places mattered.

3. Businesses should aspire to do no harm and benefit all through their products, practices, and profits.

4. To do so requires that we act with the understanding that we are each dependent upon one another and thus responsible for each other and future generations.

The path forward inspires us to achieve in the global environment of rising insecurity, fear, hate speech, and violence. There is excellent mistrust in our current economic system, and all business leaders have a responsibility and an opportunity to build a global movement of people who use business as a force for good.

This is easier said than done! One challenge is transforming the isolation and self-interest that have developed within our communities. This isolation must be replaced by connectedness, relationships, and caring for the whole. But how can this be done? Instead of focusing on society's problems, our attention needs to be on the possibilities of the community.

This transformation does not happen in isolation. We must acknowledge that we do not have all the answers as individuals. We need more than our wisdom about how to transform individually to transform a community. There is a need to create a structure of belonging that grows out of our isolated nature. Despite the view that the world has shrunk due to globalization, technology, and the ability to work anywhere, we are becoming increasingly isolated as individuals in a community.

This isolation is causing fragmentation in various sectors of our cities and neighborhoods. Our communities are separated into silos. Businesses, governments, educational institutions, nonprofit organizations, and faith-based organizations operate primarily in their worlds. A collection of programs and work operate parallel to each other. Each might be doing great work independently, but there would be much more to accomplish.

America has developed a culture of independence and individuality that, in many ways, has created this isolation and lack of interdependence. The business has developed an attitude of "go it alone," if I can make it, so can you. This culture may work for those born with the entrepreneurial spirit or given a head start because of their heritage. The challenge is to create a place that works for all, including youth, people with disabilities, people economically or socially isolated, and those growing up surrounded by discrimination for who they are or look like.

I am not here to bash the American spirit of independence and the significant advancements in technology, medicine, and science. But we must understand and acknowledge that this has left many people in our society out of many of the benefits of this advancement. The American spirit of individualism, risk, and competition is part of our story, but it doesn't have to be THE story of who America is. We must shift the narrative to the vision of what America can be. A society that cares for and embraces all of society and desires for everyone to flourish.

Our businesses can be a powerful tool to create a more inclusive economy and society. This inclusiveness will require that we listen to those who have been systematically disenfranchised over the years. Think of the people that have cried out for justice over the years. The many forms of oppression can be described as racism, misogyny, xenophobia, classism, ableism, homophobia, and transphobia. The many people who have been marginalized economically and socially cross all political spectrums and live in both rural and urban communities. People have lost trust in our systems and businesses. Most have a legitimate desire to have jobs with dignity. It is up to the business leaders to restore this trust. Economic justice for all depends on our communities coming together to ensure social and environmental justice.

Creating a sense of belonging for the marginalized is essential. When someone feels they belong, conversations can begin about how much we all have in common, leading to discussions about hospitality and generosity. Hospitality welcomes strangers to the community. Rather than feeling isolated as a new arrival in a city, the community should work to help them feel welcome. Generosity is extending an offer of help without expectations of a return on the favor. Our communities can only be transformed when these two elements are generosity and hospitality. Are actively a part of the business culture.

How Do I Engage the Community?

The key to creating or transforming a community is understanding the power of the small but essential element of building relationships. Communities are built from the gifts of the citizens. Systems can deliver services, but only relationships can provide care. Every interaction and relationship we encounter should be intentionally caring. We choose to get together to produce a desired future.

When American Express OPEN Forum encouraged shoppers to participate in a new holiday—Small Business Saturday—back in 2010, it emphasized several facts that are still valid today.

- For every $100 you spend at local, independent stores, $68 returns to your community. Only $43 stays if you spend it at a national chain.

- Independent retailers offer a unique mix of products, while national chains lean toward a guaranteed mix of popular products.

- Independent local businesses support neighborhood schools and community events with advertising dollars, while national chains rarely step in unless there's state-wide or national exposure for their ad spend.

Do these facts represent your relationship to your community as a business owner? Are you partnering with local businesses to meet your needs for products and services? Are you involved in building our local economy?

Embrace Cooperation

I agree with Kevin Leahy of Oregon's Small Business Development Center when he says, "Small businesses need to work together to compete with their larger counterparts. Only by joining forces can small businesses achieve economies of scale and have a voice loud enough to compete with larger corporations. There is power in the collective, and businesses can harness the power of togetherness to move forward in unity and accomplish so much more than they could alone."

What does this type of cooperation look like?

1. You stop looking at others who provide similar services as competitors. Instead, you recognize the benefits of knowing each other's strengths. You seek opportunities to collaborate, support, and develop profitable and rewarding connections.

2. You develop strategic partnerships where you are working toward mutual gains, such as improved customer service or better products.

3. You recognize that supporting other local businesses strengthens your community by building relationships. Whether serving a metropolitan population or a small rural community, relationship building is authentic.

4. You realize that the slight increase in the 'cost' of buying from a local business instead of the big box store or online will be offset by the benefits.

Get Active

Are you one of the businesses Ernst & Young and the Fidelity Charitable Gift Fund talk about when they report that 89% of entrepreneurs surveyed in 2011 donated money personally and through their companies? Are you among the 62% who believe "giving back makes their companies more successful in the long run?"

Beyond keeping more dollars in our community, there are additional reasons to give back benefit your business.

- When you and your employees spend time supporting community projects, feelings of well-being flow back into the workplace.

- When skills are tested and nurtured in volunteer settings, they also rebound to benefit the business.

- When employees participate in community activities, it develops more than teamwork. It may nudge hidden talents into play that you would never have discovered otherwise.

- When you are seen in the community doing something that doesn't produce profit, people find it easier to believe you are indeed in business to benefit them.

Getting active in your community can be simple.

- Contact a nonprofit you want to support. Ask if they would be interested in you placing a donation collection box in the office or your store. Would they be interested in you adding an 'advertisement' to your website at no cost to them?

- Hold a fund drive or food drive.

- Sponsor a local athletic team.

- Organize an employee volunteer day. Habitat for Humanity, a soup kitchen, or a homeless shelter are just a few ideas.

- Say yes when a school or church approaches you requesting a gift certificate or merchandise for a fundraising event.

- Accept (or seek) a volunteer position on the board of a local nonprofit whose mission you can get behind.

- Act like a local community bank that serves Seattle Metro and give your employees paid time off so they can 'volunteer' at the nonprofit of their choice.

- Spearhead an event if you see an unmet need within your community.

Start with a sustainable idea and remain open to increasing your activity within your community. In the process, you'll discover more than the rewards of being part of your local place; you'll enjoy the community as part of your life and business.

Your Community in Your Business

It's easy to slip into the "I've done all this on my own" mindset. Yet, in reality, we need help to become successful. While some of us may honestly say, "I'm a success despite everything," even then, the 'everything' inspires success. It's our community coming into our businesses every day that supports our attainments.

Infrastructure. People. Partners. Without them, business would involve significantly greater struggle.

Infrastructure

We have become so accustomed to the infrastructure in our communities that it's easy to overlook how important they are to business success. If you had to run your business in a society where these services are sporadic, you would quickly discover just how significant they are.

Infrastructure plays a significant role in economic growth. Without it, your business would face the same challenges in the developing world. As a report from the Federal Reserve Bank of Atlanta states, "The accessibility and quality of infrastructure in a region help shape domestic firms' investment decisions."

Electricity

Imagine the impact upon your business if you didn't have adequate electricity to support your technology. How would it impact customer service if you never knew when power might go out because a power station dropped offline unexpectedly? It's a minimal concern to us in Puget Sound. When we pay the electric bill, our utility companies deliver power. It takes a significant weather event to interrupt the flow.

Transportation

We pay our taxes, and Department of Transportation does more than maintain our streets and highways. Efforts continue to improve traffic flow. Highway improvements receive funds. Yes, we are the nation's fifth worst city for traffic congestion, and that is likely to stay the same, yet our roads aren't a continuous chain of poorly patched potholes.

In addition to the option of driving a personal car to work, we have the Metro system. Light Rail, rideshare programs, and bus routes also give our employees options for getting to work.

Water and Sewer

You and your employees can depend on clean water. Water-borne illness isn't likely to keep your workforce home today, and bottled water is easy to acquire if you don't like the taste.

Even if a drought forced us to conserve, our expectations of turning the tap and water coming out would remain reasonable. We expect the toilet to flush and the effluent to be adequately treated.

Phone and Internet

Our options could have been better. Cellphone towers broadcast wireless signals almost everywhere. Cables carry phones and high-speed internet signals across the region. Satellite options fill in any gaps wireless or cable lines might leave.

Every service we depend upon leverages the constancy of our infrastructure. The UPS truck driver who delivered our orders used a road to reach us and our customers. Our wireless and wired communication options empower our call and support centers, websites, and data centers.

Our Partners

In addition to our infrastructure, we depend upon others within our community to prosper. What would your business be like without the delivery services we use? Whether you use the U.S. Postal Service, FedEx, or UPS, if it's physical, it requires someone to handle its delivery.

Have you ever closed a business deal in a restaurant? They partnered with you to provide a positive experience. Have you ever used an outside venue to market your product or services? The people you worked with supported your success.

This type of partnership is so common that it's easy to overlook. Instead of thinking, "That's the least I should expect," embrace gratitude for these partners' contributions and let them know you appreciate them.

Other partners are more accessible to recognize. You could hire a payroll service to track employee benefits and paychecks. You find your business facing a challenge, so you hire someone with expertise to help you.

May I suggest you seek someone within your community who is also vested in the well-being of the place you live and work—when you reach out? Your community is already supporting your business. It's your place. It's your privilege to nurture it and let it encourage you.

Will you?

Chapter 9 - Building a Sustainable Culture of Generosity

> *"Sustainability is no longer about doing less harm. It's about doing more good." Jochen Zeitz, CEO Harley-Davidson, Inc*

Do you believe that generosity is the secret to success? In today's competitive market, a business model based on generosity can differentiate a company and build long-lasting relationships, foster a loyal customer base, and even increase revenue and profits. The way forward is simple for businesses looking to flourish while upholding the values of generosity.

Let's dive into the fascinating world of generosity and its scientific underpinnings.

1. Giving Makes Us Feel Happy. The National Institutes of Health study by Jorge Moll found that when people gave to charities, it activated brain regions associated with pleasure, social connection, and trust. Scientists believe that endorphins in the brain produce euphoria when people give to charity. A similar study out of the University of

California, Riverside, by Sonja Lyubomirsky, showed that when she asked people to perform five acts of kindness each for six weeks, participants felt more happiness than spending time on themselves. A 2008 Harvard Business School professor, Michael Norton's study found similar results even though the participants predicted the opposite would happen.

2. Giving is Good for Our Health. A wide range of research has been conducted on the correlation between giving and good health. Giving might improve our health because it helps relieve stress, which has been linked to several societal health challenges. Stephen Post wrote a book called "Why Good Things Happen to Good People" and reported that giving to others has increased health benefits for those suffering from chronic illnesses.

3. Giving Promotes Cooperation and Social Connection. The law of Reciprocation comes into play here. Several studies have shown that when a person is given a gift, they are more likely to feel compelled to reciprocate generosity. They may reciprocate to the original giver or pay it forward. These exchanges promote a sense of trust and cooperation that strengthens our ties to others. Positive social interactions are an essential factor in good mental and physical health.

In his book *Loneliness: Human Nature and the Need for Social Connection,* John Cacioppo writes, "The more extensive the reciprocal altruism born of social connections…the greater the advance towards health, wealth, and happiness." Sonya Lyubromisky writes in her book, *The How of Happiness,* "Being kind and generous leads you to perceive others more positively and more charitably. It fosters a heightened sense of interdependence and cooperation in your social community."

4. Giving Evokes Gratitude. Whether you give the gift or are the recipient of a gift, you are likely to feel gratitude. In her book Positivity, Barbara Fredrickson suggests, "When you express your appreciation in words or actions, you boost your positivity and other people's as well. In the process, you reinforce their kindness and strengthen your bond with one another.

5. Giving is Contagious. Like the law of reciprocity, when we are generous, we don't just help the recipient; we also spur a ripple effect of generosity in our community. The research of James Fowler of the

University of California and Nicholas Christakis of Harvard backs this idea up. They published the results of their study in the Proceedings of the National Academy of Science. What was remarkable about the results of their research was that generosity can inspire the recipient to behave generously later, and it could spread to more than the recipient. Your generosity may influence dozens of people you have never met.

Generosity is not just about giving; it's a pathway to personal growth and fulfillment. Your acts of generosity, whether it's sharing your time or expertise, inviting someone into your network, or empowering others with a word of encouragement, are all manifestations of your care for others and your desire to see them succeed. It's about sharing your passions and aspirations or making a positive impact. The beauty of it is that it's done with no expectation of getting anything in return but with the knowledge that you're making a difference.

Generosity is not just a feel-good philosophy; it's an intelligent business strategy. By demonstrating generosity towards employees, partners, customers, and the community, you're not only creating a positive work environment and driving revenue and profit growth in the short term, but also laying the foundation for long-term sustainable growth. Research by Fred Reichheld, the author of The Ultimate Question: Driving Good Profits and True Growth, has shown that increasing brand advocacy by 12% generates a two-time increase in revenue growth. In a world where automation is on the rise, businesses that prioritize generosity and caring in customer interactions will stand out, offering a beacon of hope for sustainable growth.

Zappos, a company that has successfully integrated generosity into its business model, serves as a beacon of hope for businesses. Their website, www.zappos.com, states their mission to inspire the world by delivering happiness to customers, employees, vendors, shareholders, and the community in a sustainable way. They believe that kindness, inclusion, and compassion are essential to business. The proof of their success? Amazon recognized the value of their generous business model and acquired them for $ 1.2 billion. This acquisition led to the creation of documents to protect the uniqueness of Zappos's culture, further highlighting the impact of generosity in business.

You may not be the next Zappos or get an offer of over a billion dollars for your business, but you can intentionally create a culture of generosity.

Embedding generosity in your business values is not just a one-time act; it's a continuous commitment.

1. Generosity as a Core Value: The first step is to make it a core value, not just a side project. This means more than just occasional charitable acts; it involves integrating generosity into every aspect of the industry, from customer interactions and supplier relations to employee treatment and community involvement. For instance, you can implement a customer loyalty program that rewards customers for their continued support or establish a supplier partnership program that offers mutual benefits. This core value can be articulated in the company's mission statement and operationalized through policies that encourage giving back, such as donating a percentage of profits to charity or sponsoring community events. Doing so changes your business and fosters more muscular, positive relationships with your customers, suppliers, and employees.

2. Foster a Generous Company Culture. Creating a company culture that encourages and rewards generosity is not just an excellent idea- it's a strategic move. By prioritizing candidates who demonstrate a spirit of giving and teamwork, encouraging employees to volunteer, providing them with time off for charitable work, and recognizing their contributions to the community, you can reinforce the importance of generosity within your company culture and reap the benefits of a more engaged and motivated workforce.

3. Provide Exceptional Customer Service. Outstanding customer service can showcase generosity. Going beyond what is expected to accommodate customers, showing genuine care and concern, and resolving issues promptly and reasonably can all be seen as acts of generosity. This can turn ordinary customers into loyal advocates for your brand.

4. Engage in Transparent and Ethical Business Practices. Trust is fundamental in any relationship; a business built on generosity will be perceived as trustworthy. This means constantly engaging in transparency and ethical business practices. Communicating openly with stakeholders, ensuring fairness in dealings, and being honest about products and services are all ways to build trust and demonstrate a commitment to integrity.

5. Build Long-Term Relationships. Rather than focusing solely on short-term gains, a generous model benefits from building long-term relationships with customers, suppliers, and partners. Building long-term relationships involves understanding and striving to meet their needs, even if it means incurring short-term costs. The return on such investments often comes from increased loyalty, more favorable terms, and positive word-of-mouth.

6. Innovate with Generosity in Mind. Innovation should focus on profit margins and consider how new products or services can benefit customers and the wider community. Innovation could involve developing environmentally friendly products, services that address social issues, or improvements that improve customers' lives.

7. Evaluate and Adjust Regularly. Finally, maintaining a flourishing business of generosity requires regular evaluation of its impact on the community, customers, employees, and other stakeholders. Evaluation involves collecting feedback, assessing various initiatives' effectiveness, and making necessary adjustments. A business owner should consider customer satisfaction, employee engagement, and the extent of community impact.

By implementing these daily actions, a business can thrive economically and contribute positively to society, building a brand that is respected and admired for its commitment to giving back.

Chapter 10 - Leaving a Lasting Legacy

"What you leave behind is not what is engraved in stone monuments, but what is woven into the lives of others." Pericles

Generosity as a Foundation

Generosity should transcend occasional gestures; it must be the bedrock of a business's ethos. Companies can make a profound difference by initiating programs that benefit the community, such as donating a percentage of profits to local charities, sponsoring local events, or offering pro bono services to those in need. These acts of generosity aid the community and build a positive brand image that resonates with customers. Moreover, businesses can inspire employee volunteerism by offering paid volunteer days or matching employee donations to charities. This encouragement fosters a culture of giving within the organization and amplifies the community's impact, leaving a legacy of goodwill.

I have one more fictional story to emphasize how generosity is good for the community and business. Over my career, I have met some great business owners and community leaders. Rather than tell a story about each one, this story encapsulates much of what I have seen and experienced.

Elevate Brews: A Business Story of Generosity

Elevate Brews is a coffee shop in the heart of the city. The company was founded by two partners who were passionate about coffee and community. They created a business that not only offered aromatic blends of coffee but also had a deeply ingrained culture of generosity. It was known in the city for a great cup of coffee and as a community hub of generosity. For instance, their donations to local schools have funded new books and supplies, and their sponsorship of community events has brought people together in celebration.

The Genesis of Generosity

Joan and Matt, the founders, began intentionally instilling a culture of excellent customer service. Every day, they met with their staff to share inspiring customer stories or brainstorm new ways to help the community. The business was more than just selling a cup of coffee. They wanted to create an environment where people felt valued and cared for.

Joan and Matt valued excellent customer service. They trained their staff to go beyond the standard level of service. Staff were empowered to occasionally waive charges for community members who couldn't afford a cup of coffee and needed a warm, safe place to hang out. They ensured their regular customers felt like they were part of a family. They were greeted by name, and their regular coffee orders were remembered and prepared the way the customer wanted. For example, they knew that one customer liked their coffee extra hot, so they always made sure to heat it a little longer for her.

Building a Culture of Giving

Elevate Brews did not just happen to have a culture of giving; Joan and Matt fostered and celebrated it carefully. They set up a program that allowed employees to take one paid day off each month to volunteer at local charities. This policy had a double impact: it supported the community and gave their staff the joy of giving back.

The coffee industry has been known for unethical practices in sourcing coffee beans, such as child labor and deforestation. Joan and Matt decided from the beginning to be transparent and ethical in sourcing their coffee. They bought from fair-trade suppliers, who ensure that farmers are paid a fair price for their beans and that no child labor is involved. They also shared stories of their growers through social media and in-store displays to educate their customers about the importance of ethical sourcing and its positive impact on communities worldwide.

Long-Term Relationships and Innovation

Recognizing the importance of long-term relationships, Elevate Brews often hosted events where local artisans could showcase their products. They opened up their café to community groups to hold meetings. This fostered rich relationships with the community and developed a strong network and supportive ecosystem.

Elevate Brews was one of the first local coffee shops to introduce biodegradable cups and offer discounts to customers who bring their mugs. However, this transition was challenging. They had to find suppliers who could meet their sustainability standards and educate their customers about the importance of these changes. But they persevered, looking at different innovative ways to help their community become a better place to live.

Reflecting and Adjusting

Joan and Matt took the time to measure the impact of their initiatives. They created reports, reviewed customer feedback every quarter, and made adjustments as necessary to maintain a strong customer—and community-oriented business. For example, they tracked the number of volunteer hours their employees contributed and the amount of money they donated to local charities. They also monitored customer satisfaction and loyalty to ensure their generosity resonated with their target audience.

A Flourishing Legacy

Today, Elevate Brews is more than just a coffee shop. It's a testament to how a business can flourish through generosity. It's a place where people come for coffee, warmth, and a sense of belonging. Joan and Matt continue to lead with generosity, and Elevate Brews is a beacon in the community. Generosity equals success!

Conclusion

Building a lasting legacy of generosity will take intentional effort. The new way of thinking about business involves being intentionally generous, collaborative, community-oriented, and connected relationally with all your stakeholders. This new way of thinking departs from the traditional business model, which often prioritizes profit over people and the planet. The new way of thinking about business is recognizing that businesses are part of a larger ecosystem and that their success is intertwined with the success of their employees, customers, and communities. Generosity to your partners, employees, customers, vendors, and local community needs to become the new business philosophy.

The foundation for generosity is built on identifying and living out your values. The five values I have lived out in my life and business are as follows.

1. Develop Authentic Relationships

2. Operating in Integrity

3. Pursue an Attitude of Service

4. Value the Individual

5. Operate in Grace

These five values are the foundation of the four stewardship principles that lead to a generous culture.

1. Stewarding Profits – How much is enough?

2. Stewarding People – Why each employee matters to business success.

3. Stewarding Partners – Create a win/win with clients and vendors.

4. Stewarding Places – Community Engagement.

Stewardship in Practice

Stewardship entails taking responsibility for the broader impacts of a business's operations, from environmental to social responsibilities. Companies should prioritize ethical sourcing, ensuring that their products or services do not adversely affect the environment or exploit labor. By implementing sustainable practices, like reducing waste, recycling, and using energy-efficient processes, businesses demonstrate a commitment to stewardship that can significantly influence local and global environments. This responsibility sets a standard for others in the industry and builds customer trust and loyalty, making them feel accountable for their actions.

Sustainability as a Strategic Priority

Sustainability is often seen in environmental terms, but it also means ensuring economic and social sustainability for a business. Sustainability involves creating both environmentally friendly and economically viable operations over the long term. For example, investing in renewable energy sources can reduce operational costs in the future while also reducing the business's carbon footprint today. Social sustainability can involve supporting initiatives that enhance education, healthcare, and equality within the community, thus contributing to a stable and prosperous local economy.

Engaging with the Community

A business that listens to and engages with its community can better tailor its initiatives to meet local needs. For Elevate Brews, this engagement takes many forms. They regularly interact with community leaders to stay informed about local issues and needs. They participate in regional forums to contribute to community discussions and decision-making. They collaborate with other local businesses and organizations on joint initiatives, such as community clean-up days or fundraising events. This engagement helps them understand their community's unique challenges and opportunities, allowing them to contribute more effectively.

Measuring Impact and Adapting Strategies

To ensure their efforts make a positive difference, businesses must measure the impact of their community-focused initiatives. This can be done through surveys, feedback forms, and community meetings. By continually assessing the effectiveness of their actions, businesses can adapt and improve their strategies, ensuring their contributions have the most significant possible impact.

Leaving a legacy in the community requires more than good intentions; it requires a strategic and integrated approach to generosity, stewardship, and sustainability. By embedding these values into every aspect of their operations, businesses can build a strong, positive reputation, foster customer loyalty, and make a meaningful impact on their communities. Ultimately, these practices contribute to a better world and enhance the business's sustainability and success.

If this message resonates with you, join my LinkedIn group, Building a Legacy of Generosity. I am available for business coaching on stewardship and speaking engagements on building a legacy of generosity.

Appendix - About the author

Art Zylstra, MBA, DTL is a seasoned and highly respected CFO. He is the founder of CFO Business Partner, a company that works with owners of for-profit and non-profit organizations to help them flourish and grow. With his MBA in Organizational Leadership and his Doctorate in Transformational Leadership, Art is well equipped to collaborate with key members of an executive team and develop and implement key strategies across the organization.

Art is highly motivated by mission and operates with integrity, confidence, professionalism, and resourcefulness. The passion that fuels Art is the understanding that when privately held businesses steward their profits, people, partners and places in extraordinary ways, the business and the community flourish.

It is Art's mission in life to help as many businesses as possible to flourish in a way that helps the community flourish. Art coaches other CFOs under the brand of The Noble CFO to extend this influence throughout the country.

Art was raised on a dairy farm in Western Washington and developed a strong work ethic that has influenced his career and volunteer work. Art has served on a variety of boards over the years in the capacity of Treasurer and President.

Art loves to travel and spend time with his wife, three children and six grandchildren. His travels have brought him to five different continents on multiple occasions.

To work with Art directly as your fractional CFO, please email ArtZ@CFOBusinessPartner.com To become a CFO under the CFO Business Partner brand or to launch your own fractional CFO practice please email the author at Art@TheNobleCFO.com For those interested in having Art speak to your company, organization or podcast please email Art at Art@StewardingYourBusiness.com.

Recommended Reading

BAKKE, DENNIS. *JOY AT WORK: A REVOLUTIONARY APPROACH TO FUN ON THE JOB*. PVG 2005

BLOCK, PETER. *COMMUNITY:. THE STRUCTURE OF BELONGING*. BERRETT-KOEHLER PUBLISHERS, INC 2018

BLOCK, PETER. *STEWARDSHIP: CHOOSING SERVICE OVER SELF-INTEREST.* BERRETT-KOEHLER PUBLISHERS, INC. 1993

COLLINS, JIM. *GOOD TO GREAT: WHY SOME COMPANIES MAKE THE LEAP AND OTHERS DON'T*. HARPER BUSINESS. 2001

COVEY, STEPHEN R. *PRINCIPLE-CENTERED LEADERSHIP*. SUMMIT BOOKS. 1991

GREEN, ROBERT K. SERVANT LEADERSHIP. PAULIST PRESS. 1977

MOHRMAN, SUSAN. *CORPORATE STEWARDSHIP: ACHIEVING SUSTAINABLE EFFECTIVENESS*, GREANLEAF PUBLISHING 2015

PINK, DANIEL H. *DRIVE:THE SURPRISING TRUTH ABOUT WHAT MOTIVATES US*. RIVERHEAD BOOKS. 2009

ZYLSTRA, ART. *THE NOBLE CFO: HOW TO START AND GROW A FLOURISHING CFO BUSINESS.* INDIE BOOKS INTERNATIONAL. 2021

Made in the USA
Monee, IL
04 November 2026

67384082R00075